Cross row style songbook for beginner

C/F diatonic accordion

Ondřej Šárek

Contents

Introduction	3
How to read tablature	3
Button Layouts G/C	4
Amcha Yisrael	5
Au clair de la Lune	7
Banks of the Ohio	9
Beautiful Brown Eyes	11
Go Tell Aunt Rhody	13
Iroquois Lullaby	14
Kum ba yah	15
London Bridge	17
Mary Had A Little Lamb	18
Michael, Row The boat Ashore	19
Oh, When The Saints	20
Old MacDonald Had A Farm	22
Oranges and Lemons	24
Reuben's Train	26
Rock My Soul	27
Shema Yisrael	28
The Cruel War	29
This Old Man	30
Tom Dooley	31
Twinkle, Twinkle Little Star	32

Introduction

Cross Row Style is often used style of playing the diatonic acordion. That´s why in this book I arranged twenty simple and familiar tunes. Each tune is available in two versions. Because the book practicing mainly right hand, left hand (bass), I arranged as simple as possible.

The book also includes chord symbols to exercise when you have a player on guitar or any instrument accompaniment. This book aims to help beginners get the necessary technique and self-confidence to not be afraid to play even harder songs.

How to read tablature

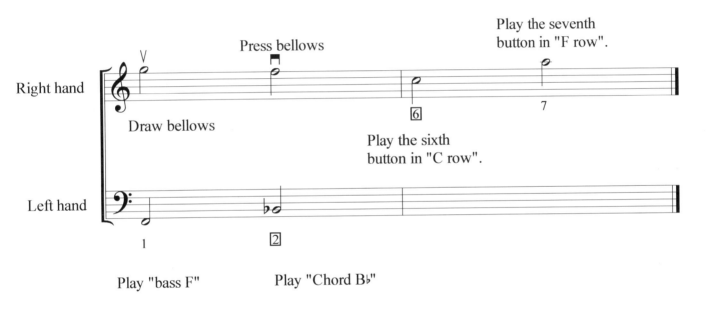

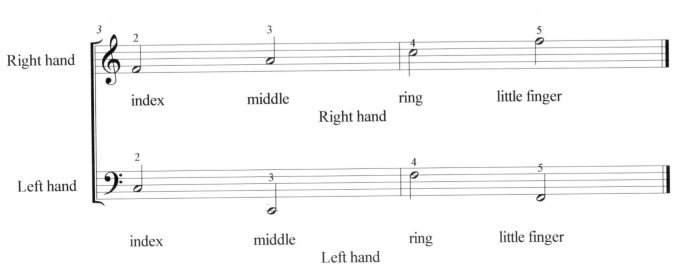

Button Layouts C/F

Score

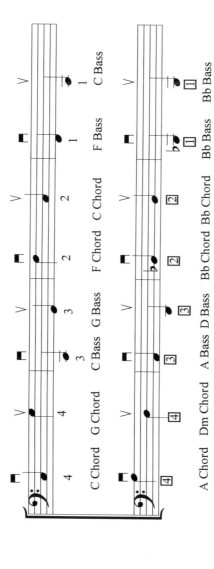
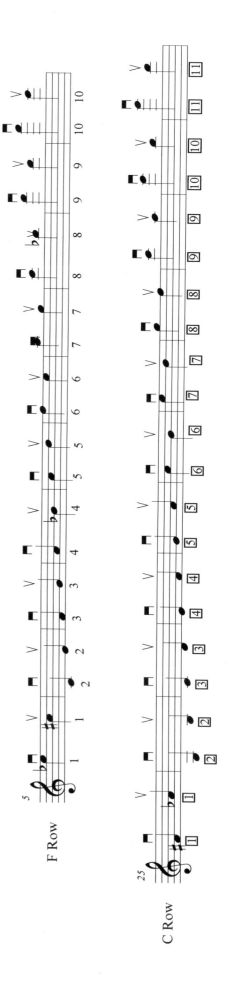

Amcha Yisrael

Yiddish
arr: Ondřej Šárek

Amcha Yisrael

Yiddish
arr: Ondřej Šárek

Au clair de la Lune

French Traditional
arr: Ondřej Šárek

Melodeon

Mel.

Mel.

Mel.

Au clair de la Lune

French Traditional
arr: Ondřej Šárek

Banks Of The Ohio

Traditional
arr: Ondřej Šárek

Banks Of The Ohio

Traditional
arr: Ondřej Šárek

Cross row style songbook for beginner C/F diatonic accordion 10 Copyright © 2013 Ondřej Šárek

Beautiful Brown Eyes

Traditional
arr: Ondřej Šárek

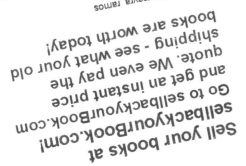

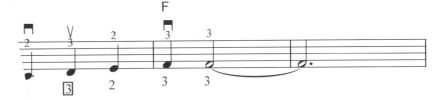

Mel.

Mel.

Mel.

Mel.

Beautiful Brown Eyes

Traditional
arr: Ondřej Šárek

Go Tell Aunt Rhody

Traditional
arr: Ondřej Šárek

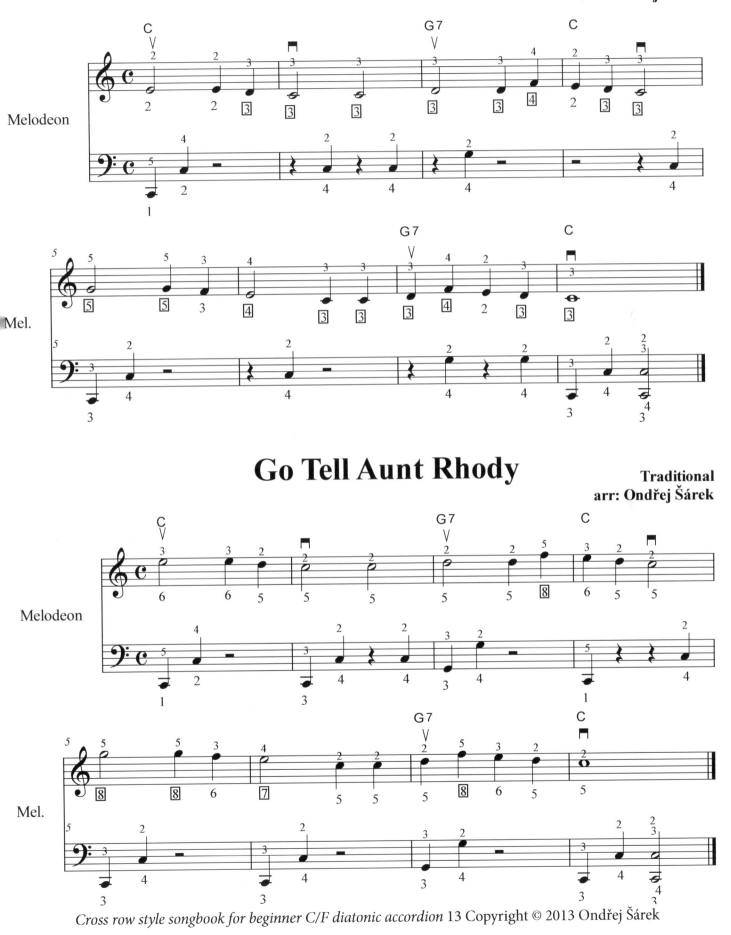

Go Tell Aunt Rhody

Traditional
arr: Ondřej Šárek

Iroquois Lullaby

Canadian Traditional
arr: Ondřej Šárek

Iroquois Lullaby

Canadian Traditional
arr: Ondřej Šárek

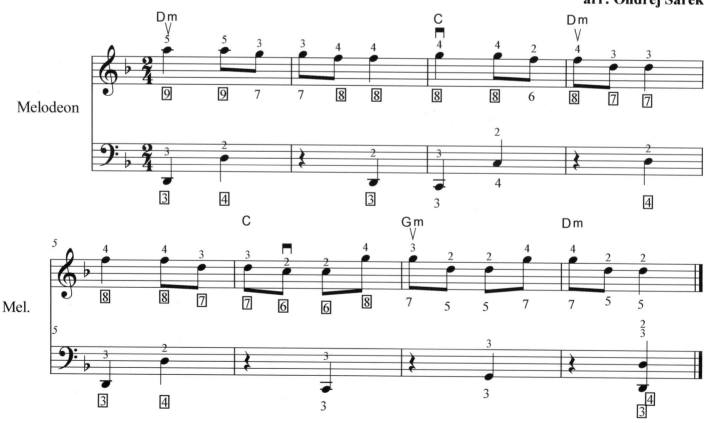

Cross row style songbook for beginner C/F diatonic accordion 14 Copyright © 2013 Ondřej Šárek

Kum ba yah

Gospel
arr: Ondřej Šárek

Kum ba yah

Gospel
arr: Ondřej Šárek

London Bridge

English Traditional
arr: Ondřej Šárek

London Bridge

English Traditional
arr: Ondřej Šárek

Mary Had A Little Lamb

Traditional
arr: Ondřej Šárek

Mary Had A Little Lamb

Traditional
arr: Ondřej Šárek

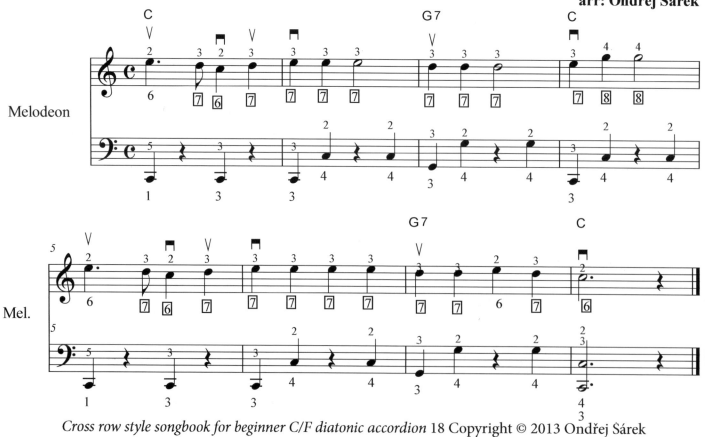

Michael, Row The boat Ashore

Gospel
arr: Ondřej Šárek

Melodeon

Mel.

Michael, Row The boat Ashore

Gospel
arr: Ondřej Šárek

Melodeon

Mel.

Cross row style songbook for beginner C/F diatonic accordion 19 Copyright © 2013 Ondřej Šárek

Oh, When The Saints

Gospel
arr: Ondřej Šárek

Oh, When The Saints

Gospel
arr: Ondřej Šárek

Old MacDonald Had A Farm

Traditional
arr: Ondřej Šárek

Score

Old MacDonald Had A Farm

Traditional
arr: Ondřej Šárek

Score

Oranges and Lemons

English Traditional
arr: Ondřej Šárek

Melodeon

Mel.

Mel.

Mel.

Oranges and Lemons

English Traditional
arr: Ondřej Šárek

Melodeon

Mel.

Mel.

Mel.

Reuben's Train

Traditional
arr: Ondřej Šárek

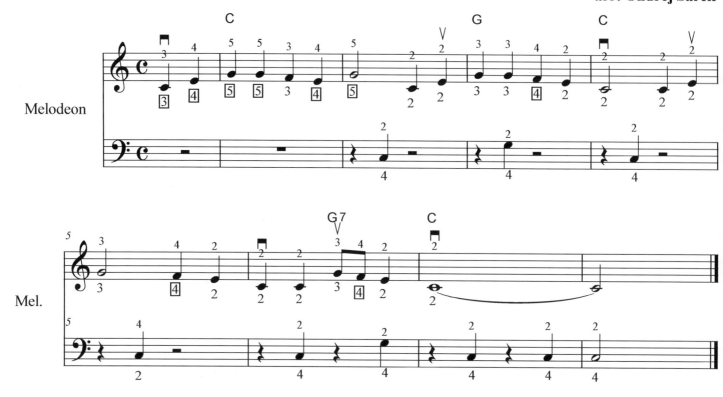

Melodeon

Mel.

Reuben's Train

Traditional
arr: Ondřej Šárek

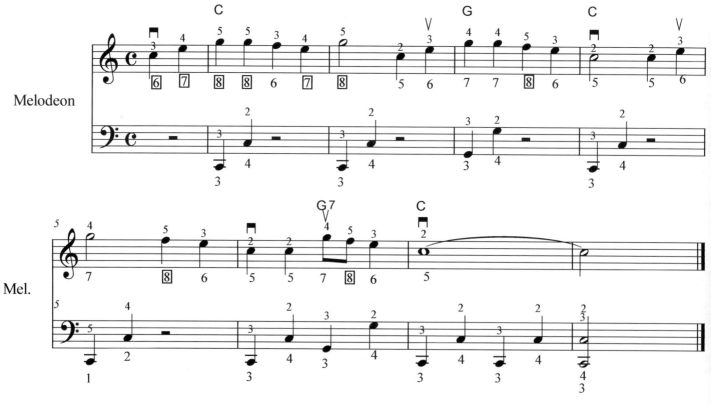

Melodeon

Mel.

Rock My Soul

Gospel
arr: Ondřej Šárek

Rock My Soul

Gospel
arr: Ondřej Šárek

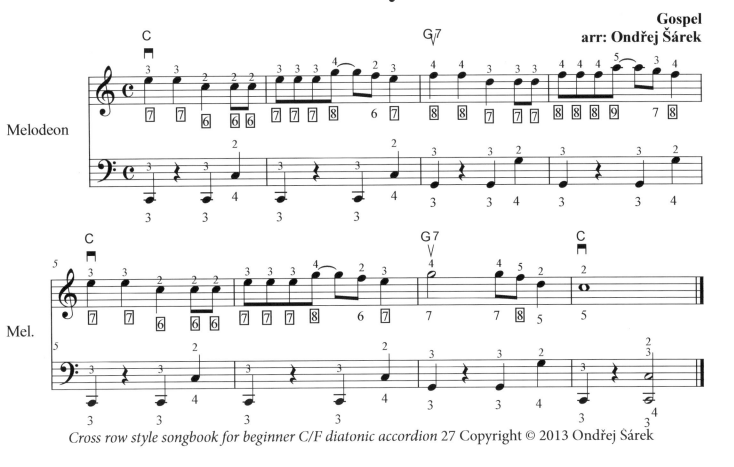

Cross row style songbook for beginner C/F diatonic accordion 27 Copyright © 2013 Ondřej Šárek

Shema Yisrael

Yiddish
arr: Ondřej Šárek

Melodeon

Mel.

Shema Yisrael

Yiddish
arr: Ondřej Šárek

Melodeon

Mel.

Cross row style songbook for beginner C/F diatonic accordion 28 Copyright © 2013 Ondřej Šárek

The Cruel War

Traditional
arr: Ondřej Šárek

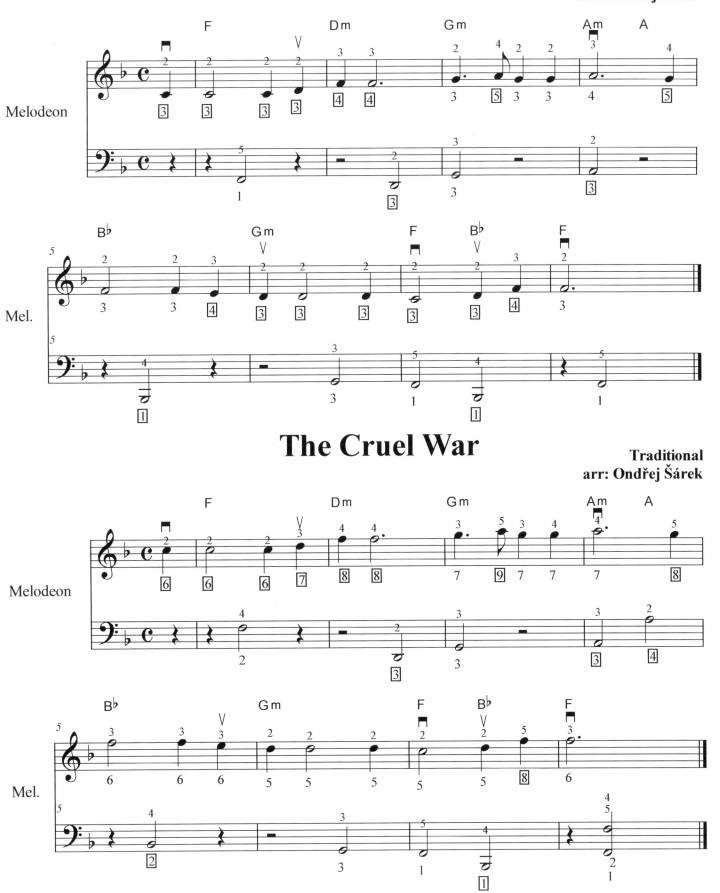

The Cruel War

Traditional
arr: Ondřej Šárek

This Old Man

Traditional
arr: Ondřej Šárek

This Old Man

Traditional
arr: Ondřej Šárek

Tom Dooley

Score

Traditional
arr: Ondřej Šárek

Melodeon

Mel.

Tom Dooley

Score

Traditional
arr: Ondřej Šárek

Melodeon

Mel.

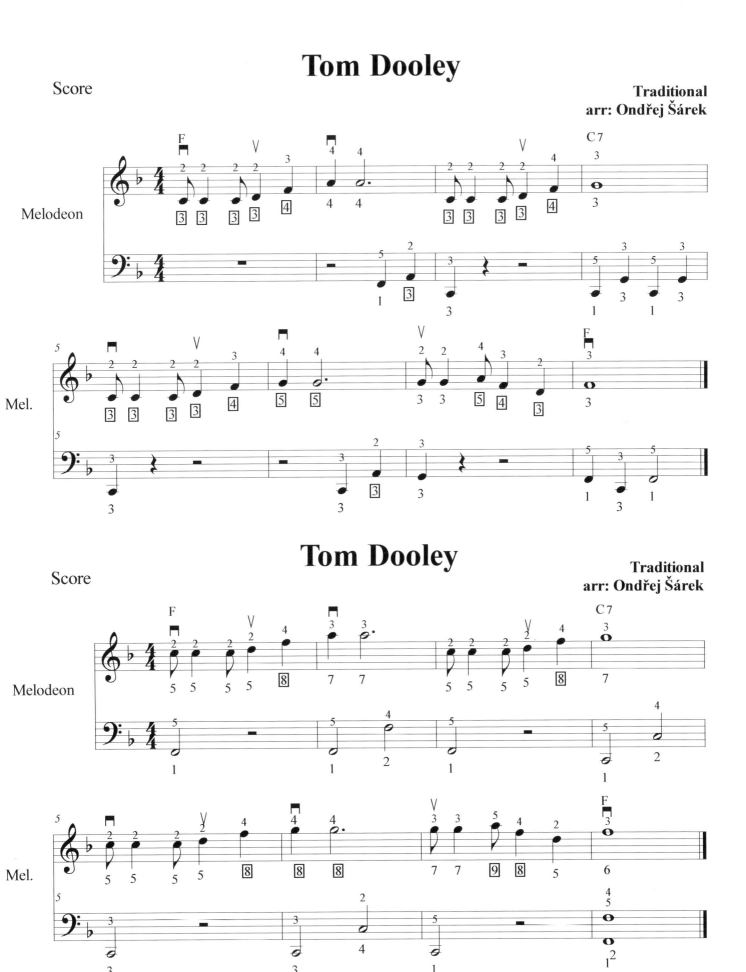

Cross row style songbook for beginner C/F diatonic accordion 31 Copyright © 2013 Ondřej Šárek

Twinkle, Twinkle Little Star

Traditional
arr: Ondřej Šárek

Cross row style songbook for beginner C/F diatonic accordion 32 Copyright © 2013 Ondřej Šárek

Twinkle, Twinkle Little Star

Traditional
arr: Ondřej Šárek

New Anglo Concertina books

For C/G 30-button Wheatstone Lachenal System
Gospel Anglo Concertina Solos (CreateSpace Independent Publishing Platform)
Notebook for Anna Magdalena Bach and Anglo Concertina (CreateSpace Independent Publishing Platform)
Robert Burns songs for Anglo Concertina (CreateSpace Independent Publishing Platform)

Coming soon!
The Czech Lute for Anglo Concertina (CreateSpace Independent Publishing Platform)
Gregorian chant for Anglo Concertina (CreateSpace Independent Publishing Platform)

For C/G 20-button
Gospel C/G Anglo Concertina Solos (CreateSpace Independent Publishing Platform)
Robert Burns songs for C/G Anglo Concertina (CreateSpace Independent Publishing Platform)

Coming soon!
Gregorian chant for C/G Anglo Concertina (CreateSpace Independent Publishing Platform)

New Diatonic Accordion (Melodeon) books

For G/C diatonic accordion
Bass songbook for G/C melodeon (CreateSpace Independent Publishing Platform)
Cross row style songbook for beginner G/C diatonic acordion (CreateSpace Independent Publishing Platform)

For C/F diatonic accordion
Cross row style songbook for beginner C/F diatonic acordion (CreateSpace Independent Publishing Platform)

For D/G diatonic accordion
Cross row style songbook for beginner D/G diatonic acordion (CreateSpace Independent Publishing Platform)

Ukulele Duets

Notebook for Anna Magdalena Bach, C tuning ukulele and C tuning ukulele (CreateSpace Independent Publishing Platform)
Notebook for Anna Magdalena Bach, C tuning ukulele and Ukulele with low G (CreateSpace Independent Publishing Platform)
Notebook for Anna Magdalena Bach, C tuning ukulele and Baritone ukulele (CreateSpace Independent Publishing Platform)
Notebook for Anna Magdalena Bach, Ukulele with low G and Ukulele with low G (CreateSpace Independent Publishing Platform)
Notebook for Anna Magdalena Bach, Ukulele with low G and Baritone ukulele (CreateSpace Independent Publishing Platform)
Notebook for Anna Magdalena Bach, Baritone ukulele and Baritone ukulele (CreateSpace Independent Publishing Platform)

New Ukulele books

For C tuning ukulele

Classics for Ukulele (Mel Bay Publications)

Ukulele Bluegrass Solos (Mel Bay Publications)

Antonin Dvorak: Biblical Songs (CreateSpace Independent Publishing Platform)

Irish tunes for all ukulele (CreateSpace Independent Publishing Platform)

Gospel Ukulele Solos (CreateSpace Independent Publishing Platform)

Gregorian chant for Ukulele (CreateSpace Independent Publishing Platform)

The Czech Lute for Ukulele (CreateSpace Independent Publishing Platform)

Romantic Pieces by Frantisek Max Knize for Ukulele (CreateSpace Independent Publishing Platform)

Notebook for Anna Magdalena Bach and Ukulele (CreateSpace Independent Publishing Platform)

Open Tunings for Ukulel (Mel Bay Publications)

Robert Burns songs for ukulele (CreateSpace Independent Publishing Platform)

Jewish songs for C tuning ukulele (CreateSpace Independent Publishing Platform)

Campanella style songbook for beginner: C tuning ukulele (CreateSpace Independent Publishing Platform)

For C tuning with low G

Irish tunes for all ukulele (CreateSpace Independent Publishing Platform)

Gospel Ukulele low G Solos (CreateSpace Independent Publishing Platform)

Antonin Dvorak: Biblical Songs: for Ukulele with low G (CreateSpace Independent Publishing Platform)

Gregorian chant for Ukulele with low G (CreateSpace Independent Publishing Platform)

The Czech Lute for Ukulele with low G (CreateSpace Independent Publishing Platform)

Romantic Pieces by Frantisek Max Knize for Ukulele with low G (CreateSpace Independent Publishing Platform)

Notebook for Anna Magdalena Bach and Ukulele with low G (CreateSpace Independent Publishing Platform)

Robert Burns songs for ukulele with low G (CreateSpace Independent Publishing Platform)

Jewish songs for ukulele with low G (CreateSpace Independent Publishing Platform)

Campanella style songbook for beginner: ukulele with low G (CreateSpace Independent Publishing Platform)

For Baritone ukulele

Irish tunes for all ukulele (CreateSpace Independent Publishing Platform)

Gospel Baritone Ukulele Solos (CreateSpace Independent Publishing Platform)

Antonin Dvorak: Biblical Songs: for Baritone Ukulele (CreateSpace Independent Publishing Platform)

Gregorian chant for Baritone Ukulele (CreateSpace Independent Publishing Platform)

The Czech Lute for Baritone Ukulele (CreateSpace Independent Publishing Platform)

Romantic Pieces by Frantisek Max Knize for Baritone Ukulele (CreateSpace Independent Publishing Platform)

Notebook for Anna Magdalena Bach and Baritone Ukulele (CreateSpace Independent Publishing Platform)

Robert Burns songs for Baritone ukulele (CreateSpace Independent Publishing Platform)

Jewish songs for baritone ukulele (CreateSpace Independent Publishing Platform)

Campanella style songbook for beginner: Baritone ukulele (CreateSpace Independent Publishing Platform)

For Baritone ukulele with high D

Jewish songs for baritone ukulele with high D (CreateSpace Independent Publishing Platform)

Campanella style songbook for beginner: Baritone ukulele with high D (CreateSpace Independent Publishing Platform)

For 6 sting ukulele (Lili'u ukulele)

Gospel 6 string Ukulele Solos (CreateSpace Independent Publishing Platform)

Gregorian chant for 6 string Ukulele (CreateSpace Independent Publishing Platform)

Notebook for Anna Magdalena Bach and 6 string Ukulele (CreateSpace Independent Publishing Platform)

Robert Burns songs for 6 string ukulele (CreateSpace Independent Publishing Platform)

For Slide ukulele (lap steel ukulele)

Comprehensive Slide Ukulele: Guidance for Slide Ukulele Playing (CreateSpace Independent Publishing Platform)

Gospel Slide Ukulele Solos (CreateSpace Independent Publishing Platform)

Irish tunes for slide ukulele (CreateSpace Independent Publishing Platform)

Robert Burns songs for Slide ukulele (CreateSpace Independent Publishing Platform)

For D tuning ukulele

Skola hry na ukulele (G+W s.r.o.)

Irish tunes for all ukulele (CreateSpace Independent Publishing Platform)

Jewish songs for D tuning ukulele (CreateSpace Independent Publishing Platform)

Campanella style songbook for beginner: D tuning ukulele (CreateSpace Independent Publishing Platform)

Made in the USA
San Bernardino, CA
30 August 2018